THE
WEST SOMERSET
RAILWAY

Volume 2

·A PAST and PRESENT COMPANION·

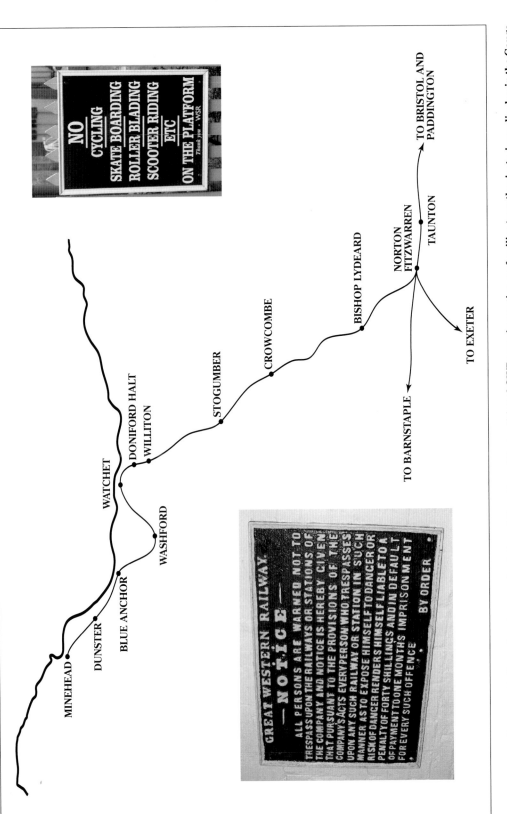

Map of the West Somerset Railway. Inset are contrasts in public notices. The traditional GWR warning notice, so familiar to enthusiasts, is on display in the Gauge Museum at Bishops Lydeard. The modern WSR equivalent can be found at the entrance to Platform 1; though they would have heard of cycling, one wonders what images skate boarding and roller blading might have conjured up for passengers of the GWR era... *DJW*

THE
WEST SOMERSET
RAILWAY

Volume 2

· A PAST AND PRESENT COMPANION ·

*Another nostalgic trip along the whole route
from Taunton to Minehead*

David J. Williams

· RAILWAY HERITAGE ·
from
The NOSTALGIA Collection

First published in 2009

British Library Cataloguing in Publication Data

A catalogue record for this book is available from the British Library.

ISBN 978 1 85895 258 1

Past & Present Publishing Ltd
The Trundle
Ringstead Road
Great Addington
Kettering
Northants NN14 4BW

Tel/Fax: 01536 330588
email: sales@nostalgiacollection.com
Website: www.nostalgiacollection.com

Printed and bound in the Czech Republic

Half title **This typical train of the British Railways era on the Minehead branch consists of a '5101' Class 2-6-2T as motive power, with a train formation consisting of a 'B' set plus a corridor coach. This view shows the 12.47pm Williton to Minehead service pulling away from Williton with No 4117 in charge.** *Graham Warburton*

Below and below right **Views showing the start and end of a journey on the Minehead branch. Class 35 'Hymek' No D7087 is seen at Taunton with a Minehead to London (Paddington) working during the 1960s, while Western Region 'Mogul' 2-6-0 No 5327 is pictured awaiting departure from Minehead during 1951.** *Peter Triggs/the late Owen Mogg, courtesy of Peter Triggs collection*

Past and
Present

A Past & Present book
from
The **NOSTALGIA** *Collection*

ACKNOWLEDGEMENTS

No project such as this could come about without the assistance of many other people besides the author, and I would like to thank the following for their help, large or small, with this book; their contribution was important and very much appreciated: Ian Aldridge, Chris van den Arend, Peter Barnfield, Ian Coleby, Peter Darke, Cedric Dunmall, Stephen Edge, K. Greenwood, Nick Jones, Steve Martin, N. H. Pankhurst, Alan Price, Allan Stanistreet, Jeff Treece, Peter Triggs, Graham Warburton, Tony Whitby, David A. Williams and John Wood.

CONTENTS

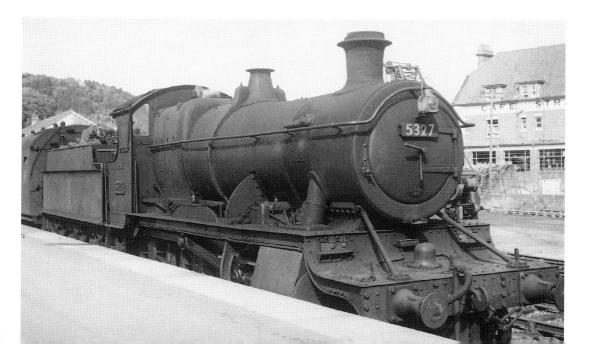

No 2996 *Victor* hauled the first passenger train on the West Somerset Railway's reopening day, 28 March 1976, suitably bedecked with ribbons and Union flag. At 10.00am Lord Montague of Beaulieu blows the whistle and waves the flag to send the inaugural special on its way from Minehead to Blue Anchor; a round trip to Blue Anchor then cost 50p. No 6412 was the other locomotive in traffic on that day, but when the 21st anniversary of the opening dawned, the Pannier was being overhauled. Visiting Pannier tank No 7760 from Tyseley Locomotive Works was the most appropriate available choice to deputise for 6412, and the loco is seen in the second photograph carrying the Union flag, bunting and 21st anniversary celebratory wreath in March 1997. Lord Montagu's son is performing the honours on this occasion, aided by the Watchet Town Crier, the Right Honourable Tom King (now Lord King), Member of Parliament for Bridgwater, and Company Chairman Dennis Taylor. Of the two locos in action on the opening day, *Victor* is now based on the Lakeside & Haverthwaite Railway and No 6412 on the South Devon Railway. *Eric Rowlands/DJW*

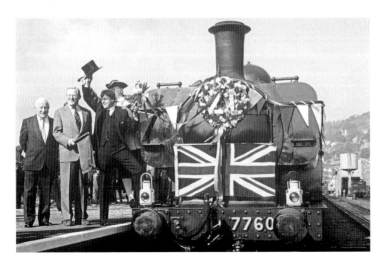

INTRODUCTION

Welcome to the second 'Past and Present' volume dedicated to the former Minehead branch of British Railways. Opened to Watchet in 1862 and between Watchet and Minehead in 1874, the line was built respectively by the Bristol & Exeter Railway and the Minehead Railway, and would eventually come under the control of the Great Western Railway, and later British Railways (Western Region). Closure came on 2 January 1971, and there followed a lengthy five-year struggle to reopen the line as a preserved, or heritage, railway.

Although the preserved West Somerset Railway has run between Bishops Lydeard and Minehead for the majority of its existence, for many, traditionally, the trip to Minehead would have started from either Taunton (usually) or the interchange at Norton Fitzwarren, where trains left the main line and headed onto the branch. Therefore, for completeness, and bearing in mind that the aims of the earliest campaigners to reopen the branch envisaged running services to and from Taunton, these stations are included in our journey. Taunton has again started to thrive, with its island platforms reopened in 2000, but Norton Fitzwarren went into rapid decline and today few (if any) traces can be found of this once large and busy station.

It was not an easy task to follow the first volume, and the biggest problem was deciding how to make the follow-up slightly different from the original, besides including different pictures. Therefore, as well as some of the older pictures of the branch in days gone by, there are also quite a number included here showing the changes that the branch has undergone since closure back in 1971. Some of the changes have been startling, and it is amazing how just a few years can alter the backdrop of a scene so dramatically. Nothing illustrates this quite so much as the approach to Minehead station since the early 1990s, where first a level crossing was installed, then the land opposite the signal box rapidly changed use from a stone unloading ground, to a flat and empty piece of land, then to a full-blown housing estate by 2005. Although not directly connected to the railway, these developments inevitably impact on both the ambience and appearance of the line itself – it is much harder to recreate a heritage line with a late 1940s/early 1950s feel to it against the backdrop of modern buildings and roadside furniture. I have deliberately not drawn a specific 'line in the sand' between 'past' and 'present', as change has been ongoing over the years, and in order to effectively illustrate what has happened at certain times an amount of flexibility has been required; some scenes remain largely unaltered over many years, while others change on an almost yearly basis.

The preserved West Somerset has really sprung into the wider public consciousness in the last 15 years, and it is easy to think that nothing much happened before then. That, though, is far from the case. The venture was certainly not an overnight success story, and many challenges faced those who took on the task of reopening the line in the 1970s. The initial aim of running a passenger shuttle, at least between Minehead and Blue Anchor, was achieved on 28 March 1976, with Williton being reached on 28 August of the same year, Stogumber on 7 May 1978 and Bishops Lydeard on 9 June 1979. That would not be the end of the struggle, as the early 1980s would bring difficult financial times that would prevail for several years. While survival was the key, the railway was improving all the time, with associated groups gradually bringing locomotives and rolling stock closer to the day when they would re-enter service and the public gradually becoming aware of the line and the beautiful scenery through which it passed.

Norton Fitzwarren was effectively the interchange station for the Minehead branch (and the line to Barnstaple), though it is hard to imagine that such a large station could once have existed on the site, for there is little trace of it today. Here we see No 4900 *Saint Martin*, the pioneer 'Hall' Class locomotive, passing through with a goods working during the 1950s, heading for Taunton. The original station dated from June 1873, though it was heavily rebuilt in 1931 as a result of the massive scheme to quadruple the running lines through Taunton, Norton being at the western extremity of this work. The layout was further revised in 1937, the first parts of both the Minehead and Barnstaple branches having been converted to double track as far as Bishops Lydeard and Milverton respectively. The station closed to passenger traffic on 30 October 1961 and to general goods traffic on 6 July 1964, though the works of Taunton Cider adjacent to the station site would continue to receive trains until the early 1990s. *The late Owen Mogg, courtesy of Peter Triggs collection*

'Hymek' No D7063 is seen on the Norton Fitzwarren section of the Minehead branch with the 13.35 Taunton to Minehead (ex-Carmarthen) service on 14 August 1965. This section of the branch was converted to double track in 1936, opening in this form from 8 June of that year, and being singled by British Railways in March 1970. *The late Owen Mogg, courtesy of Peter Triggs collection*

Many of the changes on the railway itself reflect the huge success that the line has enjoyed following its difficult beginning. In 1986 and 1987 the WSR was without suitable steam motive power for much of the time, the Great Western Society at Didcot loaning its '4575' Class 2-6-2T No 5572 to bridge the gap, though then, as now, the railway was ably supplied with diesel traction courtesy of the Williton-based Diesel & Electric Preservation Group, which has made an invaluable contribution to the line over the years. Gradually the home locomotive fleet emerged with the completion of the restoration of Somerset & Dorset 7F 2-8-0 No 88 (53808), and Collett '2251' Class No 3205 arriving from the Severn Valley Railway. A railway conference on the line in 1988 led to negotiations with the National Railway Museum to bring the last steam locomotive built for British Railways, No 92220 *Evening Star*, to West Somerset for the 1989 season, a move that confirmed to the preservation movement more widely the progress that had been ongoing for a number of years. The last day of the 1989 September Gala Week also saw another milestone, with the return to service of the Association's 'Small Prairie' tank No 4561.

As visitor numbers increased, facilities that had once been more than adequate were faced with being overwhelmed. At Bishops Lydeard in particular, the sales coach, which had been sufficient for many years, had been overtaken by the weight of customers and a new purpose-built shop with café area was erected during the closed season of 1995-96, opening at the March Gala of 1996. The scene beyond Platform 1 at Bishops Lydeard may again change beyond recognition from around 2012 onwards, with the recent granting of Planning Permission for a new Museum building, to be constructed alongside a major new residential and commercial development. A further chapter is currently being written at Norton Fitzwarren, with the establishment of a turning triangle, to be followed by a four-coach platform due to open in the summer of 2009, on a 37-acre site owned by the Association.

The 1996 enthusiasts' event heralded the first of what could be described as 'Mega Galas' based on historical themes, which attract enthusiasts from far and wide and fill every inch of accommodation for miles around. Then, in 1997, the railway won a contract that saw quarried stone, predominantly from Merehead and Whatley, transported from the main-line rail network along the branch to Minehead, where a major Sea Defence Project was under way. Perhaps that was the moment that the community as a whole finally realised the huge value of the asset that was on its doorstep, as thousands of lorry journeys were kept off the narrow and crowded roads of West Somerset and the stone was instead transported to an unloading site just a few hundred yards from the beach. From then on, the story was one of virtually continuous success, recognised by several national awards and the acclaim of public and

In 1976 three 'Small Prairie' 2-6-2Ts (Nos 4561, 5521 and 5542) were purchased by the West Somerset Railway Association from Woodham Brothers' scrapyard at Barry in South Wales for restoration and future use on the West Somerset Railway. All have since run on the line, though only No 4561 was retained by the Association, with 5521 going to the Dean Forest Railway and 5542 being purchased privately for use on the WSR. Here, No 4561 is pictured making its way through Taunton on the back of a low-loader, bound for Bishops Lydeard. *Graham Warburton*

A far cry from the immaculately kept trackbed of today, and an excellent example of the task that faced those determined to reopen the line during the 1970s, early volunteers take a break from the task of undergrowth clearance in 1976 at the top of Washford Bank. *Allan Stanistreet*

enthusiasts alike. It would, though, be wrong to forget that underpinning this success story is the hard work of those who battled against almost overwhelming odds to hack down undergrowth, clear track and prepare locomotives and carriages for traffic. The railway's success is the success of everyone who has strived to keep trains running, stations maintained, gardens tidy, signalling in working order, cleared the lineside, sold souvenirs and, perhaps most importantly of all, made tea!

The growth of the locomotive fleet has led to developments at the Minehead end of the line, too. In 1999 a brand new engineering facility was added to the original goods shed, which had sufficed as the line's engineering base since the reopening of 1976. This was designed by the line's Chief Mechanical Engineer Andrew Forster and is in keeping with the heritage surroundings in which it is constructed, being essentially an extension to a Grade II listed building. A functional carriage maintenance facility has been erected in the yard, a single-road structure originally designed to accommodate one coach, but soon extended to house a second. The most recent development was the installation and commissioning of the turntable in 2008; that year's Autumn Steam Gala was the first at which it was used in service, bringing a new dimension to this and similar enthusiast events. It will also allow the locos bringing in main-line specials to be turned and serviced at Minehead prior to their return journey.

Williton has also seen its fair share of changes, with two major new buildings appearing. The West Somerset Railway Association has established a restoration depot in a shed donated to the railway by Tarmac, which formerly stood at Swindon. This has been developed into an engineering works capable of overhauling the largest steam locomotives to the highest standards. Meanwhile, at the other end of the yard, the Diesel & Electric Preservation Group has established its own restoration facility, where major work is undertaken on the Group's collection of classic diesel-hydraulic locos.

Other changes have been less obvious, but no less important. These include the gradual introduction of Electric Key Token (EKT) working to replace Staff & Ticket working, the many improvements at all stations along the line, and the massive strides in resleepering and tamping to improve the permanent way.

Hopefully, this book will give an outline of some of the changes that have taken place and even, on rarer occasions, where things have stayed the same. One thing is certain – that without the commitment and dedication of the small paid staff and huge volunteer workforce, there would be no 'present' with which to compare the 'past'; it is these people who have kept, and will continue to keep, the show on the rails, and all of us who enjoy the West Somerset Railway today owe many thanks to all those people for their past and continuing dedication.

David J. Williams

Taunton

No 4085 *Berkeley Castle* arrives at Taunton on 3 June 1961. The semaphore signalling is prolific, water columns adorn the end of the platforms and the background buildings look well-maintained and in good order. No 4073 entered service in May 1925 and was initially allocated to Plymouth Laira; its last depot was Old Oak Common, from where it was withdrawn in May 1962.

English, Welsh & Scottish-liveried Class 66 No 66116 passes the same spot at Taunton station on 9 January 2009 working 6C51, the 12.25 Westbury to Meldon Quarry. The platform positions are unchanged, but the water columns are long gone, and the buildings beyond Platform 5 (the furthest platform) have suffered from fire and are now boarded up. The sidings to the right of the picture have gone, and consequently so has the crossover to them and the related signalling. *Graham Warburton/DJW*

In the 1960s a Pannier tank calls at Platform 1. Today the pillars for the canopy are still in the same place, but beyond that the scene bears little resemblance to the earlier picture. The island platform canopies are long gone, as is the impressive running-in board announcing this to be the junction for trains to Chard, Minehead and Barnstaple, and advertising hoardings now occupy the centre of the island platform. A local service waits in Platform 1 as a top-and-tailed Class 67 working, led by *Arrow*, pulls away from Platform 2 with 2U14, the 11.02 service for Cardiff Central. *Lens of Sutton Collection/DJW*

No 7813 *Freshford Manor* calls at Taunton station on 2 September 1961. The locomotive is carrying the reporting number H26, which indicates that this is the 10.12am Ilfracombe to Wolverhampton service. This was a dated service that ran from 5 August to 2 September 1961 only, so the picture was taken on the last Saturday of operation. Although not confirmed, it is likely that coaches from Minehead would have been attached at Taunton for their onward journey to Wolverhampton. Set into the track at the end of the island platforms are drains for the water columns that were located on the end of the platforms, and the canopy on Platform 5, at which the train is standing, has yet to be shortened with the reduction in train lengths from up to 16 coaches to a more usual 10. *Freshford Manor* was originally a Wolverhampton Oxley engine, moving to Newton Abbot in Devon in August 1950 and to Plymouth's Laira Depot in March 1959. 'Manors' visited Taunton from time to time, but did not appear on the Minehead branch, though in preservation no fewer than three of the class are permanently based on the West Somerset Railway, with a further two having visited the line in recent years.

The present-day equivalent shows First Great Western HST Nos 43195 (leading) and 43037 (at the rear) leaving with 1A81, the 08.27 service from Penzance to London (Paddington). As mentioned, the canopy has been shortened and the drainage facilities and associated columns swept away, though the island platform is now back in use. *Graham Warburton/Courtesy of Network Rail*

Norton Fitzwarren

'Small Prairie' No 5501 is seen at Norton Fitzwarren in 1951 with a short train of cargo, believed to be esparto grass from Watchet, heading off the Minehead branch bound for Taunton West Yard, passing the Railway Hotel. At this time No 5501 would have been shedded at Taunton, part of the Newton Abbot division. Esparto grass was moved along the branch by rail until 1964.

The same location was photographed on 6 June 1990 from the footbridge, which was still in situ at that time, showing the former Railway Hotel still in good condition. West Somerset Railway Association-owned locomotives Nos 4561 and 6412 are leaving the branch, though their journey is nearly at an end, for they are collecting a main-line special from Taunton Cider, which had arrived from Manchester behind a Class 47. The two steam locos took charge of the train for a return trip to Minehead and back, which was an historic occasion, being the first passenger train from the main line in the preservation era. *The late Owen Mogg, courtesy of Peter Triggs collection/Jeff Treece*

Norton Fitzwarren is unusual in being associated with two major railway accidents, the first in November 1890, the second on 4 November 1940. In the latter, No 6028 *King George VI* (originally *King Henry II* and renamed in January 1937) was at the head of the 13-coach 9.50pm London (Paddington) to Penzance express, which was running 1 hour 8 minutes late when it arrived in Taunton station. Normally this working would have left Taunton on the Down Main line. However, behind the late-running express was a lightly loaded newspaper train, also hauled by a 'King' Class loco, which was gaining time on the express in front of it. The signalman switched the newspaper train to the Down Main and the express to the Down Relief, to allow the former, now several minutes ahead of schedule, to pass the express and continue on its way. The express duly left Taunton on the Down Relief road at 3.44am with the newspaper train passing through Taunton 1 minute later and taking the Down Main.

The signal layout leaving Taunton was unusual in that the signals for both the Relief and Main lines were located to the left side of the Down Relief line, due partly to the constraints of the track layout. The driver of the express, suffering from stress and hardship as a result of his house being damaged in air raids, and working under difficult wartime black-out conditions, mistook the clear Down Main signal set for the newspaper train for the Down Relief signal, which was at Danger against the express. Only when the two trains were running parallel did the mistake become apparent; the express, still travelling at speed though slowing, was derailed on the catch points at Norton Fitzwarren together with the first six coaches of its train. Twenty-seven passengers were killed and 75 more injured. The fireman of the locomotive was killed, though the driver survived. The horror of the accident need only be imagined.

The picture above shows the condition of No 6028 after it had been rescued from a field adjacent to the line at Norton Fitzwarren and returned to Taunton Works; it was subsequently repaired and returned to traffic, not being withdrawn from its final shed, Cardiff Canton, until November 1962. *The late Jim King, courtesy of Peter Triggs collection*

A nameplate from *King Henry II*, the name carried by No 6028 prior to January 1937, on display in the Gauge Museum at Bishops Lydeard in January 2009. It is part of a private collection. *DJW*

A GWR/Western Region 'Mogul' 2-6-0, probably No 5311, leaves the Minehead branch and enters Norton Fitzwarren station. The Railway Hotel is serving beer brewed by Arnold & Hancock of the Golden Hill Brewery at Wiveliscombe.

In 1990 the now private residence was still in good condition as a Class 47 hammers past, bearing down on Taunton. As for Norton Fitzwarren station – what station? *Graham Warburton/ Jeff Treece*

Right So why was it not possible to take an exact 'present' shot in 2009? The unfortunate answer is that in early 2009 the Railway Hotel at Norton Fitzwarren was in the condition seen here, fenced off, overgrown and only a shell of its former self. The building was badly damaged by fire on the evening of 15 January 2008, and this is all that remains today. *DJW*

The Taunton Cider Works siding is seen on 16 June 1990, with the main line to the right of the picture. Nos 6412 and 4561 have arrived to collect a special working from the main line, which was transferred to the West Somerset Railway via the Cider Works' main-line connection, the first public 'through' train of the preservation era. The Taunton Cider Company was acquired by Matthew Clark Plc, the United Kingdom division of Constellation Brands Incorporated, in 1995.

On 9 January 2009 the scene is much bleaker. The Cider Works site has been cleared in preparation for housing, which is already under construction nearer to the main road, Matthew Clark having transferred production to Shepton Mallet. There is little left to indicate the works or its rail connection, though the location can be identified by the milepost in the left foreground. The connecting line to the left, with the signal at Danger, is the now permanent connection to the West Somerset Railway. Signalling for trains coming onto the branch between the junction and Bishops Lydeard is controlled by the Panel Box at Exeter St David's. *Peter Thompson/ DJW*

Bishops Lydeard

This view of Bishops Lydeard in around 1970, looking towards Crowcombe Heathfield, shows the Booking Office on Platform 1 and the Ash Priors road overbridge.

In early 2009 the view is instantly recognisable, though the revamped nature of the signalling is immediately apparent. The station running-in board has moved (it is now on the outer wall of the former goods shed, now the Gauge Museum), making way for the Nissen hut, donated by Norman Rolt and erected during the summer of 1977 to house the Taunton Model Railway Group's layouts. The tree-line behind the bridge, though it has grown a little, is otherwise almost unaltered in shape over a period of nearly 40 years. *Graham Warburton/DJW*

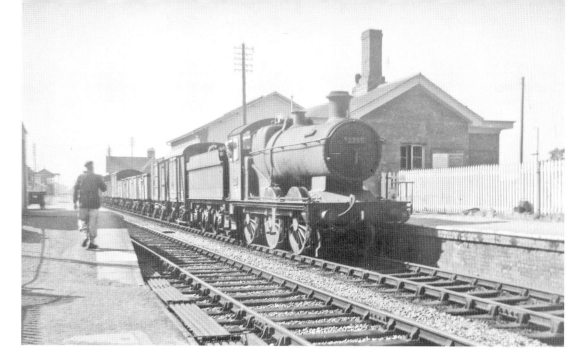

The first view shows Bishops Lydeard in 1959. A Collett '2251' Class 0-6-0 is calling with the daily pick-up goods.

In 1970, as closure draws near, the station shows little change structurally, though there is an air of decline and neglect. The railings have fallen into disrepair and the undergrowth is beginning to take hold along the platforms.

In 2009 the station has definitely lost that air of neglect. The railings have been restored and are smartly painted, and the platform furniture is immaculately maintained; a canopy now protects passengers from the excesses of inclement weather. Lighting has returned to the station building, and a telephone kiosk is preserved adjacent to the main building. Beyond the Station Master's house in the centre background is the water column. The most notable physical change from the 1970 view is the structure between the station building (to the fore) and the goods shed, which was erected during 1977 and has housed the Taunton Model Railway Group's award-winning layouts since the early days of preserved operations. A small but important feature added since the 1970s is a complex security alarm system, a sign of the times – it now takes some 20 minutes to secure the station and its environs each evening against unwanted attentions! *Peter Triggs/ Graham Warburton/DJW*

Diesel-hydraulic No D6336 arrives at Bishops Lydeard during 1964. Built by the North British Locomotive Company, the D6300s (later Class 22) were delivered from December 1958 onwards, initially as a run of six pilot locomotives, followed by a production batch that took the class total to 58 by 1962, the last surviving in traffic until 1971. No D6336 carries the split four-character headcode boxes applied to later members of the class, all the locos up until D6334 having been equipped for the disc train identification system.

By 19 September 1998 the motive power has changed as preserved Class 33 Crompton No 33048 (D6566) arrives at Bishops Lydeard with the 12.10pm Minehead to Norton Fitzwarren service. In Platform 1 Class 55 'Deltic' No D9019 is waiting to join the rear of the train to 'top and tail' the service along the Norton section, which has no run-round facilities. In its essential characteristics the station has changed very little since, save for the additional platform lighting and a more modern '1' platform indicator. The chances of seeing an Eastern Region 'Deltic' on the branch in BR days would have been nil! *Colin Caddy/Stephen Edge*

These three views were taken from the steps leading up to the Ash Priors overbridge. The first shows Bishops Lydeard in the early 1970s, in need of a flying visit from the 'Ground Force' team at the very least, and for all the world looking as though it would never welcome another train. Nowadays, of course, the railway has its own voluntary version of 'Ground Force', in the form of the Bishops Lydeard-based Restoration and Maintenance Squad (RAMS), who carry out all manner of repair work along the line, helping to keep the stations and their environs in tip-top condition.

In the centre view, taken in 1985, not only has the decay of the early 1970s been swept away, but the railway's reputation has grown to the extent that it was suggested, and accepted, as the location for filming *The Mirror Crack'd*, a BBC Television adaptation of the novel by Agatha Christie, starring the late Joan Hickson as Miss Marple. No 4561 is in shot, and No 3205 also put in an appearance.

Finally, in July 2000 the roses are blooming and the station has been transformed into the smartly kept operation that will be so familiar to visitors today. Visiting 'Black Five' 4-6-0 No 45337 is gently simmering in Platform 2, waiting to take out an evening special to Minehead. *Courtesy of Nick Jones/ Cedric Dunmall/DJW*

A different angle shows the extent of changes at Bishops Lydeard over the years. In the upper view, No 82044 is pulling away from the station and heading for Taunton; the top of the signal box can be glimpsed above the first and second carriages, and the Station Master's house (still in place today) can be seen to the left of the picture.

In the centre picture much work is afoot on 5 December 1995. The railway's aspiration to welcome longer trains from the main-line network, particularly HSTs, has led to the extension of Platform 2 beyond the signal box, while on the left of the picture new watering facilities have been provided. The station house, by now a private residence, can just be glimpsed through the supports of the water column.

Yet more changes are in evidence in this view taken in March 2004. The water column (and beyond it the Station Master's house) are the markers to the left, but the station has by now been completely resignalled, and the 'Quantock Belle' dining set is occupying its own purpose-built siding in the bay adjacent to Platform 2. The platform extension, seen under way above, is now completed, and the scene is set off nicely by '4575' Class 2-6-2T No 5552, visiting from the Bodmin & Wenford Railway. *Colin Caddy collection/Peter Thompson/DJW*

An unidentified Class 35 diesel-hydraulic calls at Bishops Lydeard during 1962, with a nine-coach train in tow; the platforms are deserted, the train ignored.

In 2000 there is again a 'Hymek' in the platform, this time No D7017, which has now been on the line for some 30 years, being one of the operational locomotives at the reopening gala held to celebrate the line reaching Bishops Lydeard in 1979. The gap between station building and goods shed has been filled by the Nissen hut and there is decidedly less 'shed' on the end of Platform 2, but beyond that the scene is not dissimilar from that nearly 40 years earlier, though trains are no longer going unnoticed and the rolling stock differs. *Colin Caddy/DJW*

Here is the Bishops Lydeard signal box and station layout as it was in 1962, with British Railways Standard 2-6-2T No 82044 departing for Taunton. No 82044 was the last of the class to be built, entering service at Barry depot in August 1955. The locomotive was based at sheds in the Bristol area between June 1958 and September 1961 and, following a month at Neyland, was allocated to Taunton depot between October 1961 and June 1964, the period in which this picture was taken. It later worked from Exmouth Junction (June 1964), Gloucester Horton Road (May 1965) and, reinstated from store, Bath Green Park in October 1965. The loco's lined black livery with unlined coal bunker and numbers displayed below the cab windows was unique for the class. Members of the class based at Taunton would also have worked services on the Barnstaple branch in 1962 while the line's turntable was out of commission, while Bristol-based '82000s' would have worked to Taunton and Minehead, particularly during the winter of 1958. With a new '82000' Class project having been launched at the Severn Valley Railway, it is conceivable that one of these locos could one day visit the Minehead branch again.

The view in the mid-1970s shows the platform and signal box and the fairly rudimentary facilities then available on Platform 2; note also how the track layout has altered since the 1960s. The signal box was closed on 1 March 1970, the same day that the box at Norton Fitzwarren was taken out of commission. At this point the section ran from Silk Mill Level Crossing (just outside Taunton, replaced by a road overbridge in 2005) to Williton.

A few months after completion, in September 1996, the platform is now extended beyond the signal box, which is how the layout appears today. Beyond, further down the platform, the present Association retail establishment and buffet can be seen; this facility, which succeeded the sales coach that had in turn superseded a Siphon G based in the goods shed yard, was opened for the Spring Steam Gala of March 1996, and sports an impressive *King John* weathervane (after the shop's retail manager, John Pearce), made by WSR volunteer Harry Kirkland.
Colin Caddy/Graham Warburton/DJW

This 1980s view shows No 6412 and a background devoid of railway furniture, other than that awaiting a home as part of future projects.

No 6412 had a long association with the West Somerset Railway, having been sold to the WSR by the Dart Valley Railway in 1976 and being moved between the two lines under its own steam along the main line. The 1934-built locomotive shared services with No 2996 *Victor* on the first day in March 1976 and spent three periods in traffic, between 1976 and 1978, 1984 and 1993, and 1997 and 2007. It was sold to the South Devon Railway and transferred to Buckfastleigh by road on 8 January 2009. The locomotive also had the honour of hauling the opening train on the Dart Valley Railway (now South Devon Railway) on 5 April 1969; the DVR had purchased the locomotive, together with two other members of the class, direct from BR the 1960s.

The view that passengers and visitors see today includes the distinctive water column now in residence. Visiting 4F Class 0-6-0 No 44422 is demonstrating the facilities. *Jeff Treece/DJW*

Crowcombe Heathfield

The first of these two views of Crowcombe Heathfield station was taken in the early 1970s, the second in 2008, and the contrast could not be more marked. The most obvious, of course, is the immaculate state of the station in 2008 compared with what was rapidly becoming a jungle in the early 1970s. The second chimney has disappeared from the station waiting room in the later view and there is no longer the pointwork for the siding leading into the loading bay, this having been removed. The state of the track today is immaculate, and new buildings have emerged on both platforms – the hut from Flax Bourton station on the Bristol to Exeter line, which closed to passengers on 2 December 1963, is located beyond the running-in board on the up platform. A signal box, waiting room (erected on site by Buildings Bespoke of Hereford) and greenhouse are on the down platform, together with a rail display and concrete signal post with signal, commissioned on 10 May 1994 as part of the resignalling that included the signal box and passing loop. *Graham Warburton/DJW*

In 1970 Crowcombe Heathfield station looks a bit of a wreck and, in common with many other buildings on the line at the time, is deserted and derelict.

In the centre view we have moved on to October 1978, when Southern TV dressed up Crowcombe station to be home to the Carter Family for the second series of *The Flockton Flyer*. A concrete screen shielding the entrance to the gentlemen's toilet from view was judged rather unsightly, and this was covered up with the white weatherboard lean-to seen on the Taunton end of the station building. Note that the window frames and the paling fence at the Minehead end of the up platform have been spruced up by Southern TV, whereas the fence at the Taunton end of the station building is in rather more dilapidated condition. Two 'prop' lamp-posts have also been added by the television company. *The Flockton Flyer* was a children's television serial that ran to two series (12 episodes), helping to put the fledgling preserved West Somerset Railway on the map, and starring '64XX' Class 0-6-0PT No 6412 in the title role. It was released on DVD in March 2009 together with a 24-page accompanying booklet, and will doubtless be available from either Minehead or Bishops Lydeard station shops during your visit.

By December 1982 the station looks much improved, structurally sound and well-maintained as Hudswell Clarke 0-6-0T No 1731 *Jennifer* arrives with a seasonal dining special. The 1942-built locomotive, formerly Stockbridge Railway No 20, arrived on the West Somerset Railway on 20 November 1982 from the North Yorkshire Moors Railway, but after the 1983 season was out of traffic for a variety of reasons, and shots of it in traffic are therefore considered quite rare nowadays! The loco remained on the line until 16 July 1993. *Graham Warburton/Nick Jones/ Stephen Edge*

Despite being located at the summit of the line, Crowcombe Heathfield often floods during the winter months, as water runs off the hills and rapidly fills drains and ditches. Here the National Railway Museum's 'Super D' 0-8-0 No 49395 enters the station with a train for Bishops Lydeard during the March 2008 Spring Steam Gala, with water rising towards the top of the rails.

The second view shows Crowcombe Heathfield as it is today, photographed in the rather more temperate weather conditions of early January 2009. The running-in board now displays the full title of the station, and behind it is the new addition to the station buildings, the disabled toilet facility, making the station one of the best-equipped on the line. *Both DJW*

The decision to reinstate a signal box and crossing loop at Crowcombe Heathfield dates to the late 1980s, with the installation being commissioned on 10 May 1994. Its purpose was to increase line capacity during galas and the peak season timetables. A new signal box had been sought by the station's volunteers to replace one that had been destroyed by fire in the latter stages of the British Railways era, and this was to be built on the foundations of the previous box. The chosen cabin was transferred from Ebbw Vale Sidings South in South Wales, where it had latterly been employed as an office rather than a signal box, and upon arrival by road on a low-loader was stored on a Weltrol wagon in the siding of the former loading bay (now removed) until the brick base and locking room had been constructed.

The lever frame employed had 'done the rounds', having been previously used at Marsh Junction in Bristol, then moved to Frome North from 1970. The frame was purchased by the West Somerset Railway in 1984 when Frome North closed. Some of the new signals were designed in the style of the originals, which had square-section posts and wooden arms. The current layout allows the signal box to be switched out when not required.

The operating cabin was lifted into position from its Weltrol wagon by crane and lowered onto the brick locking room in the autumn of 1990, after which the signalling for the remainder of the loop was installed. The sections between Crowcombe Heathfield and Bishops Lydeard and Williton were operated under the 'Staff & Ticket' method of operation until 5 August 2006, when Electric Key Token (EKT) working was commissioned.

The first picture (*above left*) shows work commencing on building the locking room base as the operating floor awaits installation in the siding beyond the platform. This unusual cargo was moved into the platform by Class 14 No D9551 (*below left*) ready to be lowered into position (*top right*). The fourth picture (*middle right*) shows the box in position but not yet fitted out and minus its steps, while the final view shows the signal box as it is today, in full working order. *Stephen Edge/Michael Hodge (3)/DJW*

A desolate-looking Crowcombe Heathfield station, looking towards Stogumber, is seen in the early 1970s. Undergrowth has taken hold with both tracks and the platforms rapidly being overcome by nature.

There could hardly be a more radical change in appearance and atmosphere in the 'present' view taken around 25 years later, on 29 October 1994. A weed dare not show its face on either track or platform and the potted flowers and hanging baskets are immaculately well-kept as 'Warship' Class No D821 *Greyhound* (with No D1010 *Western Campaigner* tucked in behind) enters the station with the 11.25 service from Minehead, as Class 50 No 50149 *Defiance* crosses with the 12.10 from Bishops Lydeard. Passengers and enthusiasts strain for a view, a far cry from the desertion of the early 1970s. *Lens of Sutton Collection/Stephen Edge*

The backdrops to many stations have changed, particularly in recent years, and that at Crowcombe Heathfield is no exception. When Baker's lorry yard and depot closed, a new row of houses was constructed on the site. The first picture shows the lorry depot just prior to demolition, then we see the new houses at what became Baker's Orchard under construction. *Both DJW*

Below On 13 March 1975 No 6229 *Duchess of Hamilton* was moved down the branch from Minehead at the start of its journey to Swindon and then York. The locomotive was towed by Class 25 No 25059 with a brake-van separating it and the 'Pacific'. In 1964 No 6229 had been the last locomotive to use the original turntable at Minehead when it was turned (separated from its tender) prior to going on static display at Butlins Holiday Camp. The train is seen near Roebuck Crossing, near Crowcombe Heathfield. *Peter Triggs*

Leigh Wood

Between Crowcombe Heathfield and Stogumber there are two level crossings, at Roebuck and at Leigh Wood. Both were formerly controlled by gates operated by crossing-keepers, but are now automatic.

The first view shows the crossing at Leigh Wood in 1973. In the days when the branch was operational, the gates here would have been closed across the road from when the first train of the day entered the section until the last train of the day left. Vehicles and pedestrians wishing to cross had to wait for the crossing-keeper to insert two levers in the ground frame, which set the Distant signals to Caution; there was then a 2-minute wait to ensure safe passage for any train that had already passed the Distant signals, and only then could the gates be opened to road traffic. The system was not entirely free from error, and occasionally a new set of crossing gates would

need to be ordered. Red roundels on the gates, removed by 1973, acted as stop signals for trains approaching when the gates were against them. The cottage is seen still in situ, with gates closed to the railway (which had been closed for two years by this time) and what is believed to be the former wash-house in the foreground.

In 2008 the cottage is no longer, demolished courtesy of No 6412 and a length of wire; this was a condition of reopening to Bishops Lydeard, to improve visibility for drivers using the crossing.

The third view shows the gates still in position in 1973, while in the last picture a local farmer takes his flock between trains across the automatic crossing that guards the crossing today, taking care to ensure that a man is posted on each side of the road to prevent inquisitive sheep trotting off down the line. Note the reduced vegetation on the banks beyond the crossing, a tribute to the hard work of the railway's volunteer Cutting Back Gang and several individual lengthmen who clear the line so that photographers can see in, passengers can see out and crews have good visibility of the line ahead. *Norman Solomon (2)/DJW (2)*

Stogumber

The short platform at Stogumber was extended between 1998 and 2000, largely to accommodate the increased passenger numbers visiting the neighbouring Bee World farm animal centre. The work consisted of constructing a new, separate platform in line with the original at the Crowcombe Heathfield end. This was opened and the original platform was then closed while three extra pillars were constructed to form a link between the two sections. Progress was slow because work had to be undertaken under engineering possession, difficult during the summer season, and also due to a subsidence problem that caused part of the original platform to collapse. The extension opened in spring 1999, the new platform being fully completed in spring 2000. Unfortunately Bee World closed in Autumn 2000, reducing the number of passengers boarding and alighting at Stogumber.

These pictures show the work in progress, looking towards Williton, with the new platform extension being built around the former waiting shelter (*top*), the work as completed (*middle*) and in 2008 (*bottom*), but without the former waiting shelter, which became unsafe and had to be demolished. The railway is in the process of rebuilding this structure, with work being at the foundation stage at the end of 2008. *DJW (2)/Allan Stanistreet*

In 1956, looking towards Taunton, a Prairie tank approaches Stogumber with a Minehead-bound train. Both waiting shelter and goods shed are intact, the latter clearly still very much in use. Goods facilities were withdrawn from Stogumber on 11 August 1963, the goods shed being declared unsafe and demolished around 1965. The signal box, located next to the waiting shelter, closed as early as 6 April 1926.

In 2008 the waiting shelter has gone (though only temporarily until a new one can be erected) and there is only the running line still in place, with the station picnic area located on the ground in front of where the goods shed stood, in line with the station building. The running line is now fenced in front of the station building. *Graham Warburton/DJW*

In the 'past' picture the station building at Stogumber is practically derelict, and it is hard to believe that it will one day be transformed into the fine building seen in the second view. The station here is unusual in that, due to the steep drop away directly behind the platform, the main building is on the opposite side of the line to the platform. *Graham Warburton/DJW*

Williton

In July 1961 a Pannier tank drifts into Williton from Taunton. Note the pointwork to the loop, which lasted in this form until 1967 when the loop was shortened and the pointwork moved nearer the station.

In 2006 WSR 2-6-0 No 9351 waits to enter the station with a Minehead-bound service. It is not possible for trains from opposite directions to enter the station simultaneously, so either the down (as here) or up train must wait to be called forward. *Peter Barnfield/Tony Whitby*

These three views show different eras and changing motive power at Williton. In the first, regular performer No D6336 trundles into Williton en route for Taunton in 1964.

During January 1982 an emergency local service was provided by the railway between Minehead and Williton when weather conditions became so bad that many roads in West Somerset were impassable. It also worked through to Bishops Lydeard under special dispensation from the Department of Transport in the winter of 1978 in similar weather conditions, carrying mail and medical supplies. Here No 2994 *Vulcan* is seen arriving at Williton. *Vulcan* entered service on the railway on 5 September 1977 and was, at times, the only steam locomotive in traffic. Its last trip was on 13 September 1984. Note the change in style of water columns since 1964.

Also in fairly dire weather, No 34039 *Boscastle* arrives at Williton during the Spring Steam Gala of March 1996. This was the 30th anniversary of the Somerset & Dorset Railway's closure, and for the event station names were changed to those on the former S&D route, hence 'The Pines Express' arriving at Evercreech Junction. By now, watering facilities have, at least temporarily, been abandoned! *Colin Caddy/ Stephen Edge/DJW*

In the early 1990s the West Somerset Railway Association started work on establishing an engineering and restoration base at the Minehead end of Williton station. A prefabricated, vault-roofed structure dating from 1899, which had formerly been at Swindon Works, was donated by Tarmac and erected on site during 1992. Since then, great strides have been made in equipping the shed with machinery (and engineers) capable of carrying out work of the highest quality, the team's biggest achievement to date being the restoration from scrapyard condition of rebuilt 'West Country' Pacific No 34046 *Braunton* on behalf of its private owner.

The first picture shows the site immediately prior to building work commencing, while on 20 May 1992 (*middle*) construction is in progress, with the steel frame already in position. Finally we see the site during 2008 (*bottom*) with a 'Manor' 4-6-0 awaiting a boiler lift prior to entering the works. The structure is a Grade II listed building. *Peter Thompson (2)/DJW*

This postcard view shows Williton station just prior to the First World War. It is believed to have been taken around 1912, and it features the original footbridge of 1874, which dates the picture to before March 1913, when an iron girder latticework bridge replaced the wooden structure.

In the second postcard view the station is seen during the floods of 1929; note the new footbridge since the earlier view was taken. *Lens of Sutton Collection/C. C. Hole, courtesy of Graham Warburton collection*

'4575' Class 2-6-2T No 5516, in its final year before withdrawal, is waiting in the up platform at Williton with the 12.51pm service from Minehead to Taunton on 4 March 1961.

The 'present' view shows the station as it is today, also looking towards Minehead. The track alterations of 1967 can clearly be seen, the track sharply leaving the platform at the end of the shortened loop; this occurred when a new minimum-depth bridge was installed over the stream at the Taunton end of the station and the line over it was singled. There is now no footbridge (though that formerly installed at Trowbridge is in the station car park in readiness for when funds allow it to be erected), as the structure erected in March 1913 was removed during the late 1960s. *Graham Warburton/DJW*

At 12.49pm on 20 April 1957 No 6360 is about to leave Williton with a service for Taunton.

In the same position today the locomotive would already have left the platform and pulled away towards what has, since 1967, been single track over the minimum-depth bridge between the signal box and the road overbridge. No 88 is pulling out of the loop as it leaves Williton for Bishops Lydeard. Save for the satellite dish, the house adjacent to the station is in very similar condition to that shown in the earlier view. *Graham Warburton/DJW*

Pannier tank No 4663 arrives at Williton station with the 4.30pm Minehead to Taunton working on 25 June 1957. Passing the same spot during the winter of 2008 is S&DJR 7F 2-8-0 No 88 (53808). The disc signal, catch points and platform end are virtually the same as in the earlier view, though the Swindon shed now stands to the left of the picture, together with several items associated with the WSRA engineering depot. *Graham Warburton/DJW*

Left In the first of these very differing views of the Minehead end of the Swindon shed at Williton, the land immediately behind the shed has been commandeered by a film company for an adaptation of Anthony Trollope's novel *He Knew He Was Right* for BBC Television in late August 2003: St Michelle rail terminal has been constructed from scratch in just two days, with a large number of extras hired as passengers (the novel was written before St Michelle and Susa in Italy were connected by a rail tunnel, opened in 1871). The Swindon shed itself, although just visible in this picture, did not feature in the final version, with the Alps being added digitally instead. The second picture shows the shed on an 'ordinary' day. *Both DJW*

This page Filming was not restricted to the shed area, as an internal carriage scene at London Victoria was shot in the yard (*above*) and the station itself was disguised as Lessborough (spelled Lessboro' in the novel) to appear in the adaptation (*right*). *Dinmore Manor* appeared both as a French locomotive and a loco representing Somerset & Dorset Railway motive power, its identity often disguised by exhaust from the locomotive aided and abetted by a smoke machine. Three coaches were hired from the Vintage Carriages Trust based at Ingrow West on the Keighley & Worth Valley Railway; all carried the Somerset & Dorset Joint Railway crest during filming. Perhaps the most surprising fact about the filming is that it was carried out while a normal summer timetable was operating, with only two trains affected, these having a bus replacement between Watchet and Williton. It's all in a day's work for the staff and volunteers of the West Somerset Railway! *Both DJW*

Doniford Halt

The halt at Doniford was opened by the West Somerset Railway on 6 May 1988, initially to serve the nearby Haven Holiday Centre, giving the WSR more operational stations in Somerset than British Rail at that time. In British Railways days and before, there wasn't a station at Doniford, and the halt was assembled from pre-cast concrete sections acquired from Montacute station on the Taunton to Yeovil line. The corrugated iron pagoda was retrieved from Cove on the former Exe Valley line, which closed to passenger traffic in 1963 and goods in 1964. In the upper picture No 88 (53808) calls in 1990, before the pagoda had been erected.

In 1997 a stone working rumbles through headed by English, Welsh & Scottish Railway Class 37 No 37718. The pagoda is now fully erected though awaiting painting, and the running-in board has been temporarily removed – in latter days, the station has been renamed simply to Doniford Halt, the 'Beach' having been removed. The station is a request halt, with passengers needing to signal to the train to stop if they wish to board, or inform the guard at Williton or Watchet if they wish to alight. The halt is in use throughout the main season, though in the winter and at certain galas it is not used; special timetables in use on the day specify when it is closed. *Both DJW*

On 29 May 1996 the pagoda shelter from Cove is being re-erected at what was then Doniford Beach Halt, now Doniford Halt.

By 1 August 1999 the completed pagoda is in place as No 4160 drifts by en route for Watchet. The locomotive is carrying its 1948 livery with 'British Railways' on the tank sides; having been built by the Western Region of British Railways, the '5101' Class 2-6-2T didn't carry GWR livery at any stage in its career. Note the garden now taking shape opposite the platform. *Peter Thompson/Stephen Edge*

Watchet

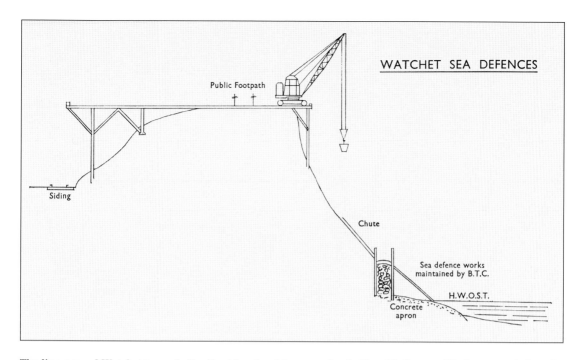

WATCHET SEA DEFENCES

Public Footpath

Siding

Chute

Sea defence works
maintained by B.T.C.

H.W.O.S.T.

Concrete
apron

The line around Watchet towards Doniford has fought an ongoing battle with the sea. Work was carried out by the Great Western Railway in the 1930s, by the British Transport Commission in the 1960s, and twice again since the line has passed into preservation. This is because of the nature of the rock in the area, which is made up of red and grey Keuper Marls, being very hard when dry but easily eroded when in sustained contact with water.

In 1962, when the first two pictures were taken, severe storms the previous winter had damaged the already installed sea defences, which consisted of a double line of rail piles installed at the bottom of the cliffs near the railway line. These had sleeper-panelled curtain walls filled with masonry topped with concrete and a concrete apron at the foot. However, the joint between the concrete and the rock became exposed by erosion, allowing water to get in, the wave action causing the concrete apron to break up into large pieces.

The foot of the cliffs were only accessible on foot at low tide by walking half a mile along the sea shore, and it was undesirable to introduce heavy lorries to the land above. The BTC therefore constructed a timber platform on trestles, which extended out over the cliff face on the seaward side and over the railway line on the landward side, as seen in the accompanying diagram. On top of this, a Jones KL22 crane was fitted, capable of moving between the two ends of its platform. At high tide, when work was not possible at the base of the cliffs, the crane would lift materials from wagons placed on the siding beneath the timber platform to form a stock-pile. The material would then be hand-fed into a mixer, also located on the platform, and the mixed concrete, partly bagged and partly loose, was lowered by the crane from the seaward end of the platform into a chute, down which it slid to the base of the cliffs, from where workers could move it into position by hand.

The photographs show the timber platform behind the train. The running line is nearest the camera with the siding on the far side, creating an impression of double track. In the upper view '6106' Class 2-6-2T No 6148 is seen approaching Watchet station with a Minehead-bound train, while below, '57XX' Class 0-6-0PT No 5779 is shunting wagons in the siding adjacent to the running line. No 6148 was allocated to Taunton between August 1961 and March 1963, when it moved to Bristol St Phillip's Marsh depot. No 5779 spent more than a decade based at Taunton shed, being allocated there from Truro in October 1950 and remaining there until moving to Bristol St Philip's Marsh in December 1961. *Both Graham Warburton*

'4575' Class 2-6-2T No 5522 enters Watchet with a Minehead-bound train during the summer of 1956. Records show that at this time No 5522 was an Exeter-based locomotive, being shedded there between September 1953 and March 1959, when it went to Taunton depot, from where it would eventually be withdrawn. Note that the signal box, although unused for some 30 years, is still in good order, and would retain its original roof until the summer of 1961. *Graham Warburton*

Left '4575' Class 2-6-2T No 5525 pulls away from Watchet in July 1961. The vehicle directly behind the locomotive is a former slip coach.

At the same location in 2004 No D1010 *Western Campaigner*, owned by the Diesel & Electric Preservation Group, pulls away from Watchet. Both sights are very much Western Region, though the sounds of a '4575' and a Maybach diesel-hydraulic differ slightly in tone! *N. L. Browne/DJW*

Right A contrast in British Railways Standard locos: in 1963 No 82044 pulls into Watchet while at the same location in 1989, in the preservation era, No 92220 *Evening Star* passes. Both views are taken from the footbridge that crosses the line at the Minehead end of the station. The visit of *Evening Star* is regarded by many as a landmark, in that it showed the extent to which the railway had progressed after its financial difficulties of the early 1980s. *Colin Caddy/Ian Wright*

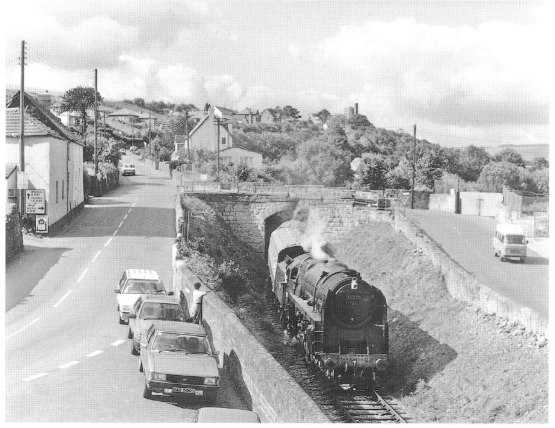

North British diesel-hydraulic No D6336 leaves Watchet for Minehead around 1963.

On 9 May 1998 a First Great Western HST pulls away from the station with a through working from the main line. The platforms at Watchet were modified around 1996 in order to accommodate through trains such as this. *Colin Caddy/Stephen Edge*

The first view of Watchet station was taken around 1965, the year in which it lost its goods facilities. The signal box, erected in 1874 with the opening of the new section to Minehead, was of Bristol & Exeter design, slightly narrower than that at Williton and built up on a 'pedestal' to give the signalman an improved view of approaching trains and of the quayside sidings. The box closed on 11 August 1926, but remained in good condition for decades, though the roof was levelled to the condition seen in this picture in July 1961; later it was completely demolished.

The second picture shows the station as it is now. The goods shed is home to Watchet Boat Museum, dedicated to telling the story of the 'flatner', a double-ended flat-bottomed boat with no keel once popular in Somerset. The additional Dutch barn-type facilities seen to the far right of the earlier picture are long gone, as is any trace of trackwork, though it is still possible to see the path of the former loop/goods siding, which passenger trains were prohibited from using. *Colin Caddy/DJW*

The station buildings at Watchet are seen in 1970, and in rather superior condition in 2008. Being the former terminus of the original line between Norton Fitzwarren and Watchet, the station building is set at right-angles to the track. Much of the transformation at Watchet in recent years is due to the continuing efforts of the Friends of Watchet Station, who raise funds for and volunteer on the station; the sign to the fore was new in 2008. Note the amount of housing development that has sprung up behind the station building on the bank overlooking the platform. *Graham Warburton/DJW*

Ex-GWR '4575' Class 2-6-2T No 5548 arrives at Watchet during 1958, and 50 years later No 6024 *King Edward I* arrives during 2008. The buildings on the far side of the road, and the goods shed, are unchanged, at least in outline, though the land adjacent to the station, which hosted sidings leading to the docks in 1958 is, in 2008, a pay and display car park. *Colin Caddy/DJW*

'8750' Class Pannier tank No 9670 waits to draw wagons away from the docks at Watchet in the early 1960s. The locomotive entered traffic in May 1948 and went directly from Swindon to Taunton, where it was based for most of its career until September 1964.

Today it is hard to believe that rails ever reached the docks, as the site is now given over to car parking in connection with Watchet Marina. Perhaps the best way of lining the two pictures up is from the edge of the dock, seen with the end of a ship moored in the earlier view, and to the left of the modern view. *Graham Warburton/DJW*

Washford

These three views of Washford over the years are looking east towards Taunton. In the first, dating from around 1960, the goods shed is still intact and in use; goods facilities were lost in July 1964 and the goods shed did not survive long after, though the sidings remained for around a further two years, locked out of use.

The middle picture was taken on the last day, 2 January 1971. The backdrop is sparse to say the least, the sidings having been lifted and the goods shed having gone some years earlier.

In 2008 the Somerset & Dorset Railway Trust's workshops and associated sidings occupy the space formerly occupied by the goods shed and yard; the workshop's main doors are from Wells (Priory Road) goods shed. Over the years there would appear to have been some slippage affecting the running-in board, probably caused by marshy ground. *Lens of Sutton Collection/Edwin Wilmshurst/DJW*

Washford station is seen just one step away from a triffid attack in the early 1970s! This desolate scene is what would have greeted the Somerset & Dorset Railway Trust in 1974-75 when it first began transferring rolling stock from Radstock. The signal box had been taken out of use on 24 August 1952 (the sidings then being worked by ground frames), and it certainly appears in a worse state than the station buildings.

Today the station is once more well-maintained and houses the Somerset & Dorset Museum, while the signal box has been renovated. *Graham Warburton/Allan Stanistreet*

The approach to Washford station from Blue Anchor is seen first in 1976, then in 2008. In 1976 No 6412 is shunting two rather forlorn-looking industrial locomotives, No 1788 *Kilmersdon* (nearest the camera) and *Henbury*. Both locos have since been restored to working order, *Henbury* at the Bristol Harbour Railway and *Kilmersdon* by the Somerset & Dorset Railway Trust at Washford.

In December 2008 No 6695, visiting from the Swanage Railway, passes the same location. The lawn effect of 2008 is a far cry from the weed-strewn wilderness of 1976, and much foliage has also been cleared from the bank on the other side of the line, allowing views across Exmoor; the fence, more distant hedge-line and tree remain almost unaltered. *Peter Triggs/DJW*

Looking towards Taunton, No 4128 is seen at Washford on Saturday 18 July 1961. More recently No 7820 *Dinmore Manor* pulls away bound for Minehead. The goods shed has been absent for nearly 40 years, but its place has been taken by the Somerset & Dorset Railway Trust's Museum workshops and associated sidings. The station differs from others on the line in having a Southern Region decor in line with S&D practice, rather than the chocolate and cream associated with the rest of the branch. *Peter Barnfield/DJW*

The motive power passing through Washford has varied considerably over the years. In August 1981 No 2994 *Vulcan* is seen rolling (or possibly rocking!) into the station en route for Williton.

By 2003 visits from the main-line network were common, and over the weekend of 10/11 May of that year Virgin Trains arranged for one of its 'Voyager units', No 220 001, to visit Minehead in order to be named *Somerset Voyager*, the railway holding a Cross Country Weekend to coincide with the event. Here the unit passes through Washford, where such a scene was perhaps not envisaged back in 1981. *Charles Kinsey/DJW*

By 1976, when this view of Washford was taken, it was becoming hard to believe that there had once been a busy goods yard and goods shed on the site opposite the platform. The Somerset & Dorset Railway Trust's project at Radstock was abandoned during the winter of 1974-75, during which period much of its rolling stock was transferred to Washford.

The second picture shows the transformation that eventually occurred and represents the site as it is today. The building to the right of the picture is the Trust's workshop, opened in 1988 and home to a number of items of rolling stock under restoration, as well as Peckett 0-4-0ST No 1788 *Kilmersdon*. *Both Allan Stanistreet*

'Small Prairie' No 5548 waits to leave Washford for its onward journey to Taunton in an undated view from the British Railways era, while in March 2004 0-6-0PT No 6412 rests in the station with an auto-train working. *Joe Moss/DJW*

'Bulldog' Class 4-4-0 No 3418 *Sir Arthur Yorke* calls at the station around 1946. Note the Starter signal – the signal box on the platform was still in use until 1952. Throughout its career No 3418 was largely associated with Worcester shed (initially) and later Reading and Southall as part of the Paddington Division.

The winter of 1977-78 was particularly harsh in West Somerset, and the railway battled through adverse weather conditions to provide emergency services, including a steam run over the as then unopened section between Williton and Bishops Lydeard. During that spell of poor weather a Park Royal DMU is seen calling at Washford in the snow. A number of S&DRT locos are stored in the recently laid sidings, including *Kilmersdon* and Ruston & Hornsby diesel shunter No 24; *Henbury* can also be seen. *A. N. M. Garry, courtesy of Peter Darke collection/Chris van den Arend*

Blue Anchor

This charming picture from the late 1950s could almost be a scene from a GWR/Western Region publicity poster, with some young passengers, buckets and spades at the ready, pictured on the down platform at Blue Anchor outside the 1904 waiting room.

By contrast, the 'present' view is on a bitterly cold December day in 2008, and enthusiasts are well wrapped up against the weather as No 6024 *King Edward I*, its support coach directly behind the tender, arrives with a Bishops Lydeard-bound service. The down platform waiting room has been the Great Western Museum since establishment by Peter and Ginny Barnfield in 1985; the canopy, which usually rests on the steel girders protruding over the platform, is temporarily absent due to winter maintenance. *Graham Warburton/DJW*

A 'Hymek' (Class 35) arrives at Blue Anchor with a goods bound for Minehead. Although the last formal workings along the branch under BR ownership are, quite rightly, associated with 2 January 1971, a Hymek-hauled 'demolition train' travelled over the line on Sunday 3 January with a formation consisting mainly of open plank wagons collecting items of railway furniture. Some local people collected their own souvenirs, including the gate wheel from Blue Anchor signal box, which was later donated back to the railway once the preservation effort was under way.

The middle view shows Blue Anchor station, again looking towards Taunton, this time around 1973 in what might literally be termed its 'wilderness years'. The scale of vegetation on the banks adjacent to the down platform would constitute a major disaster for the Station Master of today and his volunteers, who labour ceaselessly to keep the station in good order.

By 1998 the station is once more in a well-maintained and orderly condition as Class 37 No 37798 passes through with a stone train working for the Sea Defence Project at Minehead. These trains ran between 24 March and 17 December 1997, and again between 6 January and 16 June 1998; the Mainline-liveried No 37798 appeared on 22 loaded workings during that period.
WSSRT/Lens of Sutton Collection/DJW

Dunster

This is the view looking towards Blue Anchor around 1970, showing the path, 'Sound Whistle' board and, in the distance, the level crossing and signal. All track other than the main running line was subsequently lifted.

However, by October 2003 the line into the goods shed had been reinstated, now as a long siding rather than a loop as in BR days, and is seen here in use for shunting demonstrations, performed by visiting Pannier tank No 1369 from the South Devon Railway, as No 5637 arrives with a passenger service bound for Minehead. *Graham Warburton/DJW*

In the summer of 1976 No 2996 *Victor* arrives at Dunster bound for Blue Anchor. *Victor* was built in 1951 and originally went to Margam Steelworks but, together with two other similar locos, including *Vulcan*, it spent the majority of its working life at 'The Austin' at Longbridge in Birmingham, where it arrived in 1957. The signal box has led a nomadic existence, having been originally built for Hallen Marsh, between Avonmouth and Filton in the Bristol area, but not used, instead finding a home at Nelson & Llancaiach East in South Wales. It was from here that it moved to Dunster, opening on 19 March 1934 when the double-track section was commissioned between Dunster and Minehead.

In December 2008 7F 2-8-0 No 88 arrives from Minehead. Apart from the lack of signal posts and signal box, the obvious difference is that there is now a ground frame for the points leading into the reinstated goods shed siding; the running-in board, lying prostrate in the earlier view, now stands proudly. A new office building has emerged on the far side of the level crossing. *Allan Stanistreet/DJW*

The double-track section between Dunster and Minehead was effectively two separate lines signalled for bi-directional traffic, as introduced by British Railways in 1966, when Minehead signal box was decommissioned and demolished. Under WSR ownership, the connection at Dunster was taken out of use, with single-line operation being introduced between Blue Anchor and Minehead; Minehead's bay platform became inaccessible other than under an engineers' possession, when the point at Dunster could be temporarily unclipped and used – trains could not routinely change from one Minehead platform to the other.

In 1977 the layout at Minehead was remodelled, controlled by Minehead East Ground Frame, and the point at Dunster and the redundant former 'down' track between Minehead and there was recovered, the disused rails and sleepers being put to good use elsewhere on the branch. Minehead East Ground Frame allowed the use of both platforms at Minehead – the 'one engine in steam' single line could operate from Blue Anchor either to the main platform or to the bay. Once the route was set and locked by the train staff for one platform, the other side of the station was isolated from the single line, which meant that shunting could take place on the 'shut-off' side of the station while the single line was occupied. This was a great boost to operational flexibility.

In 1977 the Railways Inspectorate requested that the then unused signal box at Dunster be removed to improve visibility for motorists at the adjacent Dunster West Level Crossing. Knowing that one day a signal box would be needed at Minehead, volunteer John Francis suggested that the box should be relocated at the line's northern terminus, an idea that was subsequently put into practice. The West Somerset Railway's Special Projects Officer (and later Chairman), Hugh Perrett, suggested the idea of moving the box in one piece, and subsequently planned the operation illustrated by the accompanying photographs.

This July 1961 view looking towards Minehead shows Dunster signal box as it was in its later British Railways days, with the double-track section ending just prior to the level crossing, which saved the GWR the expense of having to modify the crossing itself when the section was double-tracked. *Peter Barnfield*

The operation, carried out on a day of extremely inclement weather on Sunday 20 November 1977, involved sliding the signal box from its position adjacent to the track at the Minehead end of Dunster's platform onto a rail-mounted cradle, constructed specifically for the purpose by the railway's engineering team. The box was slid onto and from the cradle by being jacked up and then (using hydraulic jacks, horizontally) being slid along greased rails; a close-up of this process is shown (*above left*) with, from left to right, Hugh Perrett, Brian Merrett and John Sumbler pictured. The road over the level crossing was not formally closed during the removal operation as in those days the only major traffic was fuel tankers in and out of the petrol depot adjacent to the level crossing, and they didn't operate on Sundays. *Nick Jones (2)/John Wood (3)*

Once it was securely fixed in position, the signal box, sitting on its cradle, was slowly moved to Minehead using Peckett 0-4-0ST No 1163 *Whitehead* as motive power. Built in 1908, *Whitehead* was the West Somerset Railway's first working steam locomotive and was based on the line until 1982, having spent its working life at Whitehead wire works. Peckett & Sons Ltd was a Bristol-based firm that manufactured steam locomotives until 1958.

The signal box support cradle was coupled to *Whitehead* by means of a bar – a length of rail about 10 feet long with a coupling on each end. It went over the loco coupling hook and was fixed by 'D' shackles to the cradle. This bar saw a lot of use in the early days of the West Somerset Railway, which had only one flat wagon, a CCT with the body removed. The bar came into its own for hauling the CCT about when rails were being moved around the line, as the CCT 'flat' was not long enough without being 'spaced' from the loco. Of course, extra-special care was needed when using this unorthodox method of coupling.

At Minehead the signal box was unloaded in the same manner in which it had been loaded at Dunster, and located alongside the track in readiness for when it would be commissioned on 12 April 1990 as part of a revamped layout at Minehead. *John Wood*

An automatic crossing replaced the gated crossing in 1976, immediately prior to the line's re-opening. The installation was rapidly completed, with work starting on 16 March 1976, ready for inspection on the 22nd, and operational on the reopening day, the 28th. This was a considerable achievement and is believed to have been the first such operation carried out by an independent railway. *Nick Jones*

Minehead

The first view, from the 1930s, sees an unidentified 'Small Prairie' tank simmering in the platform at Minehead prior to leaving with a branch train consisting of clerestory coaches.

The middle view finds branch regular, '5101' Class 2-6-2T No 4128, waiting to leave from the same spot in the late 1950s or early 1960s.

Finally, by way of contrast an HST unit waits to leave from the same platform in 1997 with a through working bound for the main line. It's Great Western, but not as we know it... *WSSRT collection/Peter Treloar collection/DJW*

Another contrast: the first view was taken around 1970 with a unit recently arrived at a rather shabby Minehead station, the yard devoid of rails and infrastructure and nature making an early bid to recapture the station environs.

In 2009, however, motive power is definitely 'on the up' as GWR '2884' Class No 3850 simmers in the platform having just arrived from Bishops Lydeard. The yard layout has been fully replaced (and has gone through several revisions over the years) and the water column, signalling and well-maintained track all point to an orderly and vibrant railway. *Graham Warburton/DJW*

The top view, from the 1930s, depicts a prosperous-looking goods business at Minehead. However, there could not really be a greater contrast with the middle view, taken in 1976, with much of the track lifted and what there is lying low amongst the undergrowth. Beyond the shed, the yard is in use as a car park.

By the 1990s prosperity has returned, with the engineering department's jacks in place and a well-polished locomotive on show to attract the interest of passing visitors; arguably, the building of an amusement arcade has not improved the backdrop in this more recent view... *Roger Carpenter, Roger Carpenter collection/ Allan Stanistreet/DJW*

Minehead shed makes a desolate sight in 1970, devoid of track and looking decidedly the worse for wear.

In August 1991 a rejuvenated shed forms the backdrop of a locomotive pull (No 6412 being the locomotive in question) in aid of Guide Dogs for the Blind. The shed has by now long been rail-connected again, has been equipped with a pit, and the decline of the 1970s has been arrested. Enhanced workshop facilities were added during the winter of 1987-88, and the three containers that can be seen in the background form part of that development.

In 1997-98 a two-road extension to the existing goods shed was constructed, and opened on 8 May 1998 by the company's then longest-serving employee, Don Haynes. The shed is seen here in mid-construction in March 1998.
Graham Warburton/Ian Wright/DJW

In 1990 Nos 6412 and 4561 simmer on shed awaiting their next duty.

The second picture shows that the containers have vanished, and the backdrop is now the light and appropriate two-road extension to the Grade II listed former goods shed as Nos 4160 and visiting GWR 2-8-0T No 4277 cool down following a day's work in May 1999.

Finally we see the scene as it is today, complemented by two Bulleid 'Pacifics', No 34007 *Wadebridge* (left) and No 34046 *Braunton*. The occasion is the Autumn Steam Gala of 2008, the first time the recently restored *Braunton* had appeared at one of the line's premier events. *All DJW*

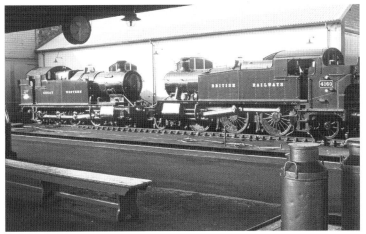

The West Somerset Railway recovered a number of substantial items from Pwllheli during 1977, including the turntable, which was by then surplus to requirements. The first picture shows the turntable being removed from Pwllheli, already in use as a mobile recruiting advertisement as it leaves the ground.

Nearly 30 years after it left Pwllheli, the turntable is lowered into the ground at Minehead on 11 February 2008 (*below*), prior to connection and commissioning during the summer. It was transported in one piece, starting its journey the previous day (Sunday the 10th) and staying overnight at Strensham services on the M5 motorway. The turntable weighs 56 tonnes and required a 157-tonne crane to lower it into position. The installation of the turntable was part of the £6 million Mart Road regeneration project in Minehead, and was jointly funded by Somerset County Council, the South West of England Regional Development Agency, the European Regional Development Fund and the West Somerset Railway.

On 13 July 2008 the turntable, dismantled into several large pieces, left the West Somerset Railway bound for Wolverhampton, where the main bow girders were extended to 65 feet in length to accommodate larger locomotives. Repairs were undertaken in the Black Country, followed by shot-blasting, painting and reassembly prior to delivery. *Steve Martin/Allan Stanistreet*

The previous Minehead turntable was installed in 1910, but being only 45 feet long it was difficult to turn 4-4-0s and 2-6-0s, a manoeuvre that involved the use of extension bars on which the locomotive's tender rested during turning. On 23 April 1957, with the extension very clearly in use, No 6360 is turned ready for its return journey to Taunton.

On 28 December 2008, during the Winter Steam Gala, No 6024 *King Edward I* is turned on the new turntable.
Graham Warburton/DJW

For many years one of the prominent features at the end of the platform at Minehead was the former Pwllheli water tower, erected under the supervision of the late Harry Lee in 1976 and seeing use up until the 1997 season. The water tower was manufactured by the Isca Foundry Company based in Newport at a cost of £100 when new; the company produced many items of 'plant' for the railways and traded until the early 1960s. The Great Western Railway opened a new (replacement) station at Pwllheli in 1909 and the tower had been situated on the station's island platform, having outlets on both sides to allow locomotives to be watered on either road.

By the mid-1990s, larger locos were in use of the West Somerset Railway and the tower was becoming too small to be of practical use. A new, larger hydraulic tower was installed much closer to the shed at Minehead, and the decision was taken to offer the ex-Pwllheli tower for sale. It was dismantled on Wednesday 20 October 1999 by Ray Lee (Harry's son) and Ray Palmer and subsequently moved to the Welshpool & Llanfair Light Railway, a move that took it back to Cambrian territory. The water tank was renovated by Welshpool & Llanfair volunteers and a specialist contractor installed a glass-fibre lining to lengthen the life of the structure. Installed in April 2001, the tower was first used in service at Welshpool (Raven Square) station on 19 May 2001.

These pictures show the tower awaiting removal from Pwllheli, with the West Somerset Railway lorry and crew in attendance (*above*), the tower at the end of the island platform at Minehead in 1997, where Loadhaul-liveried Class 37 No 37798 has just arrived with a stone working (*above right*), and No 823 *The Countess* taking water at Welshpool (Raven Square) in September 2002, with the tower now firmly back on Cambrian territory. *Steve Martin/DJW (2)*

The changing scene at Minehead is well illustrated by these three views, all looking towards The Parade from the platform. In the first, taken in the 1950s, the turntable, shed and water column are all in situ and the track is well-maintained.

By 1970 the turntable, shed and water column are no more. The well-kept track has been lifted and has give way to a weed-strewn wasteland. The background houses identify it as the same location, but the atmosphere of neglect hangs heavy.

In March 2008 it is all change. Again, the housing in the background identifies the location, but a new chapter is being written as the ex-Pwllheli turntable sits as the centrepiece of a contractors' building site, while the Railway waits for the site to be handed over so that track-laying up to the new table can begin. *Graham Warburton collection/Graham Warburton/DJW*

This undated picture, almost certainly from the late 1950s, shows Collett 0-6-0 No 2213 waiting to leave Minehead. The platform is almost deserted, something that cannot be said for the 1989 view below, as '4500' Class No 4561 attracts the attention of holidaymakers as it sets off on its journey to Bishops Lydeard. *Lens of Sutton Collection/Jeff Treece*

On 4 July 1970, 'Hymek' No D7036 waits at a weed-strewn Minehead platform with the 10.25am (Saturdays only) through working to London (Paddington).

On 13 March 1996 BR 5MT 4-6-0 No 73096, masquerading as Somerset & Dorset regular No 73052 for the purposes of a gala weekend, awaits departure with a short train. *R. F. Roberts, courtesy of Stephenson Locomotive Society/DJW*

Although both of these views are recent, and have only a few years between them, they do perhaps illustrate the speed at which the environment around the railway is changing. In September 1999 No 7820 *Dinmore Manor* rolls into Minehead with clear ground behind the train to the left of the picture, yet just four years later No 4160 passes the same spot against the backdrop of a newly built housing estate. *Both DJW*

In these sombre views of a run-down station on 31 December 1970, interested parties are reading the closure notice, and BR services have only three days to go.

By early 2009 the station is in tip-top condition, its chimneys having been replaced to replicate their appearance prior to closure and benefiting greatly from the activities of its support group, the Friends of Minehead Station, who, among other activities, run the Reader's Halt bookstall on the platform. The area around the station has been made into a pedestrian area following installation of the turntable and the addition of retail units on the adjoining land; this is the view that greets visitors and passengers today. *David A. Williams (2)/DJW*

Here are three more views illustrating the changing face of Minehead during the preservation years. In the first, volunteers are beginning the task of clearing the track during 1976. Note that none of the background features associated with the station today are apparent, other than the bank of fir trees.

The second view, taken during 1990, shows a background of railway infrastructure, with a new carriage workshop being erected to the seaward side of the line. Arriving is the Class 105 Cravens two-car DMU that arrived on the line from Derby in 1982, travelling as far as Bridgwater by rail and completing the journey by road on a low-loader. The unit is now based at Bury on the East Lancashire Railway where it is being returned to full working order.

The final view shows the workshop completed, later being extended to allow two coaches to be worked on simultaneously rather than the original one. This was a much-needed facility, for the preserved West Somerset Railway has been constantly short of undercover carriage servicing facilities throughout its period of operation. The visiting Royal Saloon is sitting outside; behind, the fir trees are still in residence!
Allan Stanistreet/DJW (2)

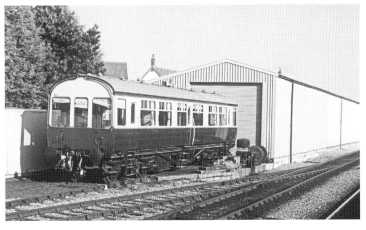

WSR locomotives

In 1976 three 'Small Prairie' 2-6-2T locomotives – Nos 4561, 5521 and 5542 – were purchased by the West Somerset Railway Association and brought to the WSR at Bishops Lydeard for restoration. No 5542 was built in 1928 and was initially allocated to Gloucester depot, entering traffic on 2 August of that year. It was very much associated with the West Country, being subsequently based at Bristol, Taunton (when it was a regular performer on the Minehead branch), Newton Abbot and finally Westbury, from where it was withdrawn on 8 December 1961. It went to Woodham Brothers' scrapyard at Barry in South Wales in February 1962, where it was to spend 14 years before being rescued and brought to the West Somerset Railway.

By 1979 the railway was struggling financially, and the sale of both Nos 5521 and 5542 was necessary. Members of the Dean Forest Railway bought No 5521 and a Taunton-based group of the line's supporters formed the 5542 Fund to purchase No 5542 for use on the West Somerset Railway. It was some 23 years before No 5542, by now based at Washford, steamed in preservation during 2002. The result of the hard work was a fine

locomotive that has worked thousands of miles since returning to traffic, both on the WSR and several other preserved lines that it has visited.

The photographs show a sorry-looking No 5542 awaiting restoration at Bishops Lydeard (*opposite above*) and the state of the bunker upon arrival (*left*). By contrast, in March 2003 the locomotive is seen leaving Crowcombe Heathfield with a Steam Recreations photographic charter and in action with Mike Little's auto-coach No 178 on the Norton Fitzwarren section of the line during the Autumn Steam Gala of October 2003. *David Cox/WSR Journal Archive, photographer unknown/DJW (2)*

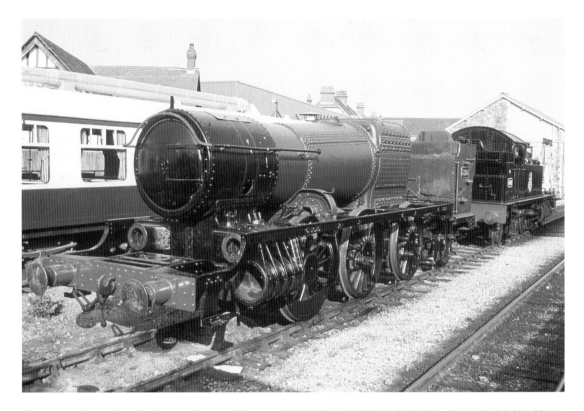

These four views show the 'past and present' forms of '5101' Class 2-6-2T No 5193. The 'Large Prairie' had been based at a number of West Country sheds during its working life, as well as spending five years at Stourbridge Junction in the West Midlands, and on withdrawal from Plymouth's Laira Depot in 1962 it was sent to Woodham Brothers' scrapyard at Barry. It was rescued for preservation in 1979 by David Rawlinson and restoration begun at Steamport, Southport, from where it was purchased by the West Somerset Railway Plc, moving from Southport to Minehead by road on 1 December 1998.

At the WSR Annual General Meeting of June 2000 a plan was announced to convert No 5193 from a 2-6-2T to a 2-6-0 tender engine. This would provide a locomotive with increased coal and water capacity and bring back to West Somerset the sight of a type of loco common to the line in British Railways (Western Region) days. It would also save manufacturing new bunker and side tanks, as the originals were beyond economic repair; the rear frames and drag box would almost certainly have also had to be replaced due to severe metal wastage.

The new WSR 2-6-0 locomotive differs from the '4300'/'9300' 'Moguls' in having a boiler that is 5½ inches less in diameter; additionally, the top of the firebox is some 6 inches lower. The side window cab is that of the '9300' Class, but the WSR loco retains the '4300'-style lever reverse.

Numbering was a subject that evoked much speculation throughout the period of the rebuild, but No 5193 emerged as No 9351, essentially its old numbers reversed by pairs, and carries WSR lettering on its cabside numberplate. The locomotive has proved itself a capable performer on the present-day West Somerset Railway and sees regular use throughout the season.

Our pictures show the locomotive as delivered to Minehead, photographed in March 1999 with No 4561 behind (*above*), the extent of decay affecting the bunker prior to removal, and the converted machine approaching Leigh Wood Level Crossing in March 2005. *All DJW*

No 7820 *Dinmore Manor* arrived at Bishops Lydeard from the Gwili Railway in South Wales in unrestored condition in 1985. Owned by Dinmore Manor Locomotive Limited, the locomotive later moved to Tyseley Locomotive Works in Birmingham for overhaul, where it was returned to steam during 1995, entering active service on the West Somerset Railway in September of that year. The loco was a mainstay of the WSR fleet for nearly a decade before being withdrawn for overhaul. No 7820 spent much of its British Railways career in the West Country, its sheds including Plymouth Laira, Truro and St Blazey. Withdrawal came from Wolverhampton's Oxley Depot in November 1965. Our views show the locomotive as it arrived on the line in 1985 and in immaculate condition at Minehead following completion of its restoration. *Peter Chatman/DJW*

Rebuilt 'West Country' Class 'Pacific' No 34046 *Braunton* was purchased by the West Somerset Railway Association in October 1995. In May 1996 it was purchased by private owner Jeremy Hosking, who financed the rebuild of the locomotive at the WSRA's engineering works at Williton. Restoration took 11 years, but when the completed loco emerged from the works in the summer of 2008, the result was quite superb. Our views show the locomotive at Bishops Lydeard in April 1996, and back in steam in 2008. The locomotive was built at Brighton Works and entered traffic in November 1946 at Exmouth Junction Shed; it was rebuilt in 1959 and withdrawn in October 1965. *Both DJW*

INDEX OF LOCATIONS

And finally, two pictures showing contrasting eras of retail activity at Minehead. In the first, though the mid-1970s were early days for the Association's retail department, it was very much a case of 'have wheels, will travel'. Volunteers Michael Grimoldby (left) and John Wood are keeping an eye open for passing punters and lurking photographers!

By 2005 the shop layout that visitors know and enjoy today has taken shape, with Mike Chilcott seen in residence behind the counter. *Both Allan Stanistreet*